Pebble® Plus

Cool Sports Facts

Cool Hockey Facts

by Kathryn Clay

Consulting Editor: Gail Saunders-Smith, PhD

Consultant: Craig Coenen, PhD
Associate Professor of History
Mercer County Community College
West Windsor, New Jersey

CAPSTONE PRESS
a capstone imprint

Pebble Plus is published by Capstone Press,
151 Good Counsel Drive, P.O. Box 669, Mankato, Minnesota 56002.
www.capstonepub.com

Printed in the United States of America in North Mankato, Minnesota
032010
005740CGF10

 Books published by Capstone Press are manufactured with paper
containing at least 10 percent post-consumer waste.

Library of Congress Cataloging-in-Publication Data
Clay, Kathryn.
 Cool hockey facts / by Kathryn Clay.
   p. cm.—(Pebble plus. Cool sports facts)
 Includes bibliographical references and index.
 Summary: "Simple text and full-color photos illustrate facts about the rules, equipment, and records of hockey"—
Provided by publisher.
 ISBN 978-1-4296-4728-1 (library binding)
 1. Hockey—Miscellanea—Juvenile literature. I. Title. II. Series.

GV847.25.C53 2011
 796.962—dc22   2009051411

Editorial Credits
Erika L. Shores, editor; Kyle Grenz, designer; Eric Gohl, media researcher; Eric Manske, production specialist

Photo Credits
AP Images/Pugliese, 17
Corbis/Bettmann, 19; Reuters, 21
Dreamstime/Rob Corbett, 9
Getty Images Inc./Bruce Bennett, 7; Len Redkoles, cover
Newscom/Icon SMI/Jerome Davis, 5
NHLI via Getty Images/Andy Devlin, 15; Bill Wippert, 13; Eliot J. Schechter, 11
Shutterstock/Peter Blazek, cover (puck), back cover, 1

Note to Parents and Teachers

The Cool Sports Facts series supports national social studies standards related to people, places, and culture. This book describes and illustrates hockey. The images support early readers in understanding the text. The repetition of words and phrases helps early readers learn new words. This book also introduces early readers to subject-specific vocabulary words, which are defined in the Glossary section. Early readers may need assistance to read some words and to use the Table of Contents, Glossary, Read More, Internet Sites, and Index sections of the book.

Table of Contents

Slap Shot! 4

Cool Equipment 6

Cool Rules 12

Cool Records 16

Glossary 22

Read More 23

Internet Sites 23

Index 24

Slap Shot!

NHL players whiz slap shots

past goalies during games.

More than 21 million fans

go to these games every season.

NHL stands for National Hockey League.

Cool Equipment

Hockey pucks are frozen

before games.

Frozen pucks don't bounce

on the ice.

Goalies wear equipment

made of Kevlar.

This same material is used

to make bulletproof vests.

A Zamboni machine smooths
the ice between periods.
The Zamboni travels a total
of 3 miles (5 kilometers)
during a game.

Welcome to the BankAtlantic Center
CLICK IT OR TICKET
FLORIDA
DANGER
LEXUS
CITY OF SUNRISE
Saveology

Cool Rules

Players can't use their sticks
to hit or trip other players.
A player who breaks
the rule gets a penalty.

Players may not

pull hair, bite, or spit.

Rule breakers get sent

to the penalty box.

Cool Records

When a player scores

three goals in a game,

it's called a hat trick.

Wayne Gretzky scored

60 hat tricks during his career.

Bobby Hull had

a fast slap shot.

He could shoot the puck

120 miles (193 kilometers)

per hour.

Teams have competed for

the Stanley Cup since 1893.

The Montreal Canadiens

have the most Stanley Cup

wins with 24.

Glossary

goalie—the player who guards the goal

Kevlar—a strong material used to make safety gear

penalty—a punishment for breaking the rules

penalty box—where a player who has broken the rules sits for a certain amount of time

period—the amount of time a hockey game is played; each hockey game consists of three 20-minute periods

puck—a small, rubber disk

Stanley Cup—the championship series of the National Hockey League; the Stanley Cup is also the name of the trophy given to the winning team

Read More

Fauchald, Nick. *Face Off!: You Can Play Hockey.* Game Day. Minneapolis: Picture Window Books, 2006.

Will, Sandra. *Hockey for Fun! Sports for Fun.* Minneapolis: Compass Point Books, 2004.

Internet Sites

FactHound offers a safe, fun way to find Internet sites related to this book. All of the sites on FactHound have been researched by our staff.

Here's all you do:

Visit *www.facthound.com*

FactHound will fetch the best sites for you!

Index

goalies, 4, 8
goals, 16
Gretzky, Wayne, 16
hat tricks, 16
Hull, Bobby, 18
Kevlar, 8
Montreal Canadiens, 20
penalties, 12, 14

penalty box, 14
periods, 10
pucks, 6, 18
slap shots, 4, 18
Stanley Cup, 20
sticks, 12
Zamboni machines, 10

Word Count: 165
Grade: 1
Early-Intervention Level: 20